# DON'T RESIST TRANSFORMATION

## TREAT CHANGE AS AN OPPORTUNITY

DHIRAJ PACHPOR

*"Offering my sincere efforts in the Lotus Feet of the Almighty"*

# Contents

*Treat change as an opportunity,*

*To step out of your comfort zone,*

*To discover new shades of yourself,*

*And to let your true colors shine.*

# Preface

In today's fast-paced and ever-changing world, the ability to adapt and transform is more important than ever. Yet, many of us find ourselves resistant to change, whether it be in our personal lives or in our careers. In 'Don't Resist Transformation', you can explore the reasons why one hold ourselves back and the ways in which one can break free from these self-imposed limitations.

Through a combination of personal anecdotes, expert insights, and practical strategies, this book delves into the mental and emotional barriers that prevent from embracing change and achieving our full potential. Whether you're seeking to make a career change, improve relationships, or simply live a more authentic life, 'Don't Resist Transformation' will offer valuable tools and guidance to help you navigate the journey towards self-discovery and positive growth.

One of the key themes of this book is that change is a natural part of life and resisting it only causes us to miss out on the opportunities that it can bring. The book also offers readers the chance to reflect on their own lives and to identify the areas in which they might be holding themselves back. The book is divided into several chapters, each of which focuses on a specific aspect of transformation. From understanding the importance of self-awareness, to learning how to set goals, and then taking action to achieve them. I also tried to share practical tips and strategies for overcoming common obstacles such as procrastination and self-doubt.

Whether you're a student, a professional, or simply someone looking to improve themselves, 'Don't Resist Transformation' could be an essential guide for anyone looking to unlock their full potential and create the life they truly desire. It's written in a way that is easy to understand and easy to apply to your own life.

# CHAPTER ONE

# KNOW THE RESISTANCE

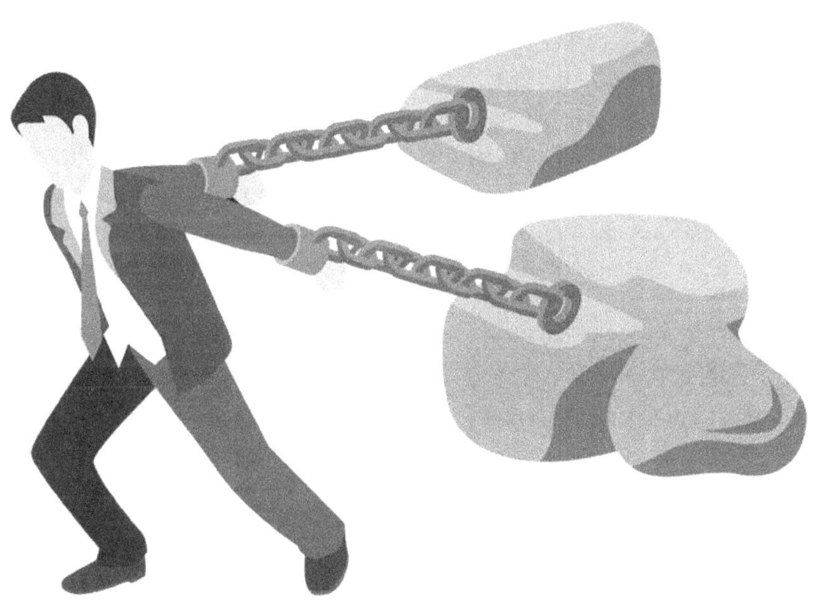

Resistance to transformation is the unwillingness of an individual to undergo some positive changes. These changes could be psychological states of mind, daily habits, ways of communicating, ways of responding and reacting, professional ethics and morals, and many other things which an individual must change or work to make it Shine. Most people, it has been noted, are resistant to change. They live with the conviction that whatever they do or practice in their daily lives is the only way to live. They are the primary practitioners of transformational resistance. Most individuals recognise the importance of change, but they expect the other person to change. When it comes to relationships, one may frequently discover that something is wrong and that something has to be changed, but the expectation of change is always from another person. The husband believes the wife should change, while the woman believes the husband should change. Friends expected each other to adjust according to their wavelength. A person working in an office maintained expectations from his employer and coworkers to change, parents consider changing their children, and children believe that their parents should change. This implies that the majority of us are sailing in the same boat, the boat of change or, more accurately, the boat of transformation, but here the transformation is anticipated to be seen in another person rather than in oneself. This thinking pattern is the most difficult to overcome and is the biggest resistance to transformation. Because the very first stage of change is identifying the need to change, But this rigid behaviour of considering oneself as perfect and expecting others to change prevents that need from developing.

We were always delighted by any change when we were kids. If someone teaches us something new, we keep repeating it and enjoying it. If we see someone doing something new to us, we try to imitate it and accept the change. It is true that it is easier to mould someone while they are younger. This is because we are more flexible and open to adapt without any fear when we are younger.

But as we grow older, we start losing our flexibility and slowly and unknowingly we started resisting transformation in ourselves, neglecting its importance to cope up with changing times. Thus as we grow younger to older, it becomes more difficult to undergo the transformation in us. The one reason for this is that as we grow, we begin to seek comforts around us, in our behaviors, in our activities, in our workplace, in our home, and gradually we bound ourselves in the fence of that comfort, which we call our comfort zone. Once the comfort zone is built, and then any transformative change is implemented, but the zone is obviously disturbed. This causes a disruption in our state of mind. Living in our comfort zone for an extended period of time creates a sense of safety in us, and the more safety-oriented we are, the more disruptions there will be with any change, resulting in greater frustration. The frustration increases with each change, and we don't even know when it reaches a saturation point and transforms into depression.

Many people find it easier to change someone else than to change themselves. They often do counseling or even manipulate others, so that they could see some transformations in others and by doing this they could easily escape from self-transformation. However, those who do this should be aware that, while it seems simple, it does not last long. As a result, it may only be a temporary solution to a lasting problem. Self-resistance to change can manifest in various forms, such as denial, hesitation, or simple rejections. These forms of resistance can be due to underlying causes, such as fear of the unknown, a lack of faith in the change process, or a loss of position or authority. For example, a person may resist changing their eating habits because they are fearful of the unknown and are unsure how to manage a new diet. They may also be concerned about the social opinions associated with change, as well as the possible loss of status or power that may occur. Another example is when a person avoids changing their professional path because they are afraid of the unknown and are unsure how to navigate a new industry. They may also be concerned about a perceived loss of status or authority, such as losing the prestige connected with their present occupation.

Driving a car forward requires a balance of acceleration and braking. If you press both pedals at the same time, you won't get anywhere as the forward motion from acceleration is counteracted by the braking effect. The same applies to transformation, it requires a forward thrust, like acceleration, to overcome resistance, which is like braking. Until the resistance is overcome, transformation cannot occur. This forward thrust is nothing but a firm willingness.Knowing and understanding resistance to change is important because it allows individuals to identify and address the underlying causes of their resistance, which can help them to overcome it and successfully navigate the change process. A story can make you understand these. long time ago, there was a warrior. He was brave and strong in battle and people respected and liked him. But even though he was successful, he wasn't happy. He always wanted to be a general and lead his army, but he kept putting it off and giving excuses to himself. He would tell himself that he wasn't ready, didn't have the support of the leader and it was too risky. His fear was resisting him to step ahead. He was scared of failing and losing the respect of others. He was also scared of leaving his known and comfortable position. But as time passed, he realized that his fear was preventing him from reaching his goals. He thought a lot about it, he came across the fact of resistance, which he was going through. One day, he decided to overcome resistance and do something about it. He became brave and asked the leader for the opportunity to lead his army. The leader was impressed by his courage and agreed. He led his army to many victories and people respected him even more. He finally became a general, and his long-time dream came true. He realized that it was his resistance to change that held him back all this time. From then on, he took risks and embraced change. He became one of the most successful generals in the history of china. He learned that facing his fears and taking action was the key to achieving his goals.

# CHAPTER TWO

# GET AN ESSENCE OF TRANSFORMATION

We have been reading, listening, and learning that 'the only thing which is constant is change.' Many people always misinterpreted the 'change' in the context of the physical world. While thinking so, we always miss the fact that we ourselves are the biggest and most important part of the world around us. So as we think of change in the world around us, how could we skip changing the self? There is a need to understand the term self-transformation, as it is essential to live a frustration-free life. Transformation is a journey that requires self-awareness, determination, and a willingness to step out of your comfort zone. It's about letting go of old habits and beliefs that no longer serve you and embracing new perspectives and ways of being. In order to get an essence of transformation, you must first understand the reasons why you want to change and what you hope to achieve. This understanding is the foundation that will guide you throughout the process of transformation. Transformation..... the word seems very deep and has a very broad canvas of context within it. Many times when we go through the term 'transformation of self' we feel that it is a complete spiritual term, and is the most difficult thing to do which generally the spiritual practitioners and monks do. But it is not true. In very simple terms it is nothing but making some positive changes in self and being willing to accept the positive change around us.

Transformation is a continuous term, which means there is always a scope for betterment in us. We can not claim easily that "yes! I am completely transformed now" because if we undergo any transformation at the same instant we may need to fix some other things in us. for example, If someone has worked on time management, it does not indicate that the scope of future adjustments has been closed. He may also need to focus on other aspects such as good communication, humility, and so on. A human being is surrounded by infinite shades of thoughts and acts, thus each moment of life is different from every other moment. That is why the way of dealing with every situation is also different. This keeps the wheel of transformation always rolling and makes its scope never-ending. Whenever you will ask a question to yourself that, "Is there a need of changing for me?" the answer is always "yes", it hardly matters what is your age, what is your profession, or what you are expecting from life. The answer to this question will always be a big yes. Just like computer software updations, every time something better version is available after each update.

The transformation of a butterfly is a good example of a transformational journey. It starts as a small and unimportant caterpillar living on the ground and eating leaves. But over time, it starts changing and slowly becomes a beautiful and graceful butterfly that can fly. This change, called metamorphosis, is not easy but it makes the butterfly strong and majestic. This transformation is not easy at all, as the process has many stages, the caterpillar first makes a cocoon around itself, where it is hidden and protected while it undergoes the changes needed to become a butterfly. It's a time-consuming process, and also the process of transformation is not just outer, but also inner that is mental, and emotional. The caterpillar must let go of its old way of life and accept a new identity as a butterfly. Similarly, the butterfly must let go of its old way of life and embrace a new one, that of flying and pollinating. The butterfly must learn to navigate new environments and understand its role in the ecosystem.

This change of butterfly acts as a reminder that change is not always easy, but it is needed for growth and development. It teaches us that even the smallest things have the potential to come out with something extraordinary. And that the journey of transformation is worth it in the end. Thus, this serves as an inspiration for us to accept change and transform ourselves for the better. It teaches us that the beauty of transformation is in the process of becoming, not just in the outcome. And as the butterfly flies, it reminds us to keep moving forward, to keep growing, and to never give up on our journey of transformation.

Another question may arise in your mind, how long it will take for someone to undergo any transformational change? the answer is it will take time, it is not at all an overnight journey that you sat on a train at night and when you wake up in the morning, you are at your destination. No, it's not like that. it's just like a small kid learns to walk. he starts with very small baby steps, but he falls several times again continues with the baby steps, and after consistent efforts and practice the kid can then walk and run. Similarly, transformation is the process of those baby steps taken slowly-slowly and making it a habit and a part of your existence. A very good friend of mine was very shy and always had a fright to interact with new people and to be expressive in mass. after so many discussions with him, he shows the willingness to change and deal with this fright of him. He started speaking to himself by seeing in the mirror, and he started speaking to people around him. But step by step slowly, it took about a month to just overcome the fear of transformation and then weeks to work on it. Now no one meeting with him can say that they are interacting with a person who was very shy, less expressive, and frightened to interact. We need to understand the role of time in this journey and should respect it. If we don't, then being impatient will take us nowhere.

In essence, transformation is a journey of self-discovery and growth. It requires us to be open to change, to take responsibility for our lives, and to be willing to put in the work required to achieve our goals. It's a process that requires patience and perseverance, but the rewards of a more fulfilling and authentic life are well worth the effort.

# CHAPTER THREE

# Overcome the Fear of Transformation

Fear is one of the root causes of resistance. There is a common human tendency of accepting the self as its favorite. Thus, when it comes to making some transformations in behavior, habits, and way of living life, the mind finds it difficult and the feeling of losing something.... losing the so-called self gives birth to fear.

Remember if you won't change, the situation will change and the changed situation will make you change, but that will be forced change and thus not a transformation. Now the question may arise that how come this change is different, and why can't we say it a transformation? to get an answer, first we need to understand the basic difference between forced change and transformation. It could be easily understood by an example of an egg. When the egg is been broken forcefully from the outside we will get the egg yoke this is a forced change from a whole egg to an egg yolk to eat. But now when the egg is as it is in the required conditions then after a particular time the egg will be broken from the inside by a baby chick, now that is a transformation from the egg into a life. A positive change that is internal and done willingly and most importantly with the acceptance of the heart is the transformation and will last forever. those positive changes which you accept from the heart are easy to adopt and easy to practice. You will feel like those habits were always with you from a long time and flows with blood in you. this could happen only when one undertakes a journey from resistance to acceptance.

Another reason for fear could be doubting own potential. "Ohh... it is so difficult, how could I do it?" or "will I be able to change?" or "transformation, seems something very extraordinary process and I am an ordinary person. how i could do it?"
These questions are nothing but excuses given by you to your subconscious mind. If it is done again and again in the loop it means you are feeding this concept to your subconscious mind and unknowingly training it in this way. Once it gets trained, your mind will always find it difficult to undergo a transformation and thus fear will be always there.

People who resist much also have a fear of adoption. They are the ones whose adaptive skills have been sleeping for a long. They have forgotten to adapt the things, situations, and surrounding. People belonging to these group imagines themselves as transformers, and they feel we need to transform everything, every situation and surrounding as per our comfort and our thought process and as usual, called by others as a dominating person. But ...... here they make a little mistake, the mistake of assuming the situations and surrounding as weak and that they could easily dominate the same being rigid. Thus as an outcome, not every time situation will change according to him, It makes such people restless, frustrated, and unhappy. They always complain about life and always remain unsatisfied. you can hear them saying "why is this happening to me?" or "why always me, god?". You may see them playing blame games. whenever something goes wrong they will be blaming to someone or something. It is just like an unskilled carpenter spoils the entire furniture and when he is asked for an answer, he blames his tools. this mentality is a resistance... resistance to transformation.

One story that illustrates the importance of overcoming the fear of transformation is the story of the rebirth of the Eagle. This story is about an eagle, after living a long life, reaches old age and finds that its feathers have grown old, the beak has a bend and its talons lose the ability to grab. The eagle begins to feel that its time has come to die.

But one day, the eagle was with beautiful feathers and a sharp beak. The old eagle realizes that to become young, it must first let go of its old self and accept death. The eagle overcomes its fear and flies to the top of a mountain and sheds its old feathers, allowing them to be carried away by the wind. He breaks the bent beak by making it strike on stone. The eagle then waits patiently for new feathers and beaks to grow. As the new feathers grow, it can fly once again. The eagle then realizes that to be reborn, it had to overcome its fear of transformation. The story may be real or maybe fictitious but the moral of it is strong enough to build willpower to overcome the fear of transformation.

Another story that I found intresting to illustrates the importance of overcoming the fear of transformation is of a college going boy.

A college boy named Amit and his friends decided to climb a mountain having a fort at its peak. They were amazed to see the huge number of people doing the fort trek and decided to join in. They quickly started and soon reached the top.

However, Amit spotted another fort on the nearer mountain that only a few people were attempting to climb. He suggested to his friends that they should also try climbing it, but they were hesitant, seeing that the path was too difficult. But, Amit took this as a challenge and set out to climb the peak alone. After just two hours, he reached the top and was greeted with applause from the other climbers who had already reached the top. Amit was happy and took in the beautiful views.

During a conversation with the climbers, Amit asked why only a few people attempted to climb the peak despite the fort here is very huge and beautiful. The climber replied that most people are content with what is easy and do not want to take risks, as they fear losing what they already have. He explained that to reach new heights, one needs to put in the effort to overcome the fear of doing something new and have courage.

Amit thanked him for the valuable lesson on the importance of courage in life. He realized that being part of the crowd and not taking risks can lead to a life of complaints and missed opportunities. With courage, one can achieve great things and reach new peaks.

Let us see some activities that can help to overcome the fear of transformation:

**Visualization:** Imagine yourself successfully making the change you desire by closing your eyes. See yourself in the new role, environment, or situation and focus on the positive feelings and emotions associated with it.

**Start with small steps:** Divide the change process into small and simple steps. This will help to focus on one thing at a time and make the change less overwhelming.

**See the change as an opportunity:** Many of us think of change as a threat and if there is any threat it is normal human tendency to experience fear, it may be less or more. But instead of viewing the change as a threat, try to see it as an opportunity for growth and development.

**Educate yourself:** Gather as much information as you can about the change you wish to undergo in you, and try to understand it from all perspectives. This can help to reduce feelings of uncertainty and fear, as the more knowledge, the less will be fear of accepting it.

**Get out of your comfort zone:** Challenge yourself to go for new things and take small risks. This can help to build confidence and strength.

**Accept feedback positively:** Seek feedback from others, and be open to constructive criticism. One of the causes of fear to change is thinking about, "what people will say?" If we start accepting feedback and criticism positively, it will help in reducing the fear. This can also help you to identify areas for improvement and make the change more successful.

**Try relaxation techniques:** Try techniques such as relief exercise, yoga, or meditation to help you stay calm and focused during the change process.

# CHAPTER FOUR

# LIVE WITH GRATITUDE

**Gratitude** is a beautiful emotion that evolved consciously when someone feels thankful for any act. If we feel that someone has done something for us through his actions, his gestures, or his words, then he should be acknowledged for it. But we always need to understand, just having a feeling of gratitude and not expressing it, is just like you love someone but can't express it, It won't work at all. the act of expression makes our feelings fly gently and reach the heart of another person, then and only then there will be the exchange of emotions. A student learns throughout the year, attends all the sessions, studies sincerely, and accumulates all the knowledge that he should be as a student. But on the day of the exam, he was supposed to write the answers, if he fails to do so, no matter how knowledgeable he is he can never pass the exams. Simply storing knowledge or emotions and not expressing them is just like a plastic apple, you can't eat it, and thus just a showpiece. Similarly, imagine a professor who is having degrees in his field of education and has tremendous knowledge, but instead of expressing that knowledge in class he just wonders and expects students should automatically learn the concept from him. But How it is possible? of course not. Expression is just like fuel to the vehicle of your emotions, it can only transfer when it is been expressed whether by words or any action.

It is most commonly seen around us, many of us do carry the emotions of gratitude toward many other people who are contributing to make our life go fine, but we resist ourselves to express those emotions of thanking. Gratitude is the easiest way to connect with the act of expression. you can be more expressive in your life if you start with it. Because while expressing gratitude you can just with a single word.....that is thank you. Gradually after some time when you start feeling comfortable then you can go ahead with praising the good action of the other person for which you thanked him. For example, if you are thanking your taxi driver you can say, " thank you, friend, you are doing a good job. Driving in huge traffic and keeping your cool is a tough job." that's set, just you moved on from one word to a sentence but its impact increase by multiples. The driver will be also receiving these positive vibes which he will be spreading throughout the day to whoever he will meet. Thus, your single act of expressing gratitude will contribute in making the world full of positive vibes.

Once a simply dressed up small boy was standing on a street with black eyeglasses and a board in his hand. The board was written with the words "I am blind, please help me with some money". He was having a cap kept in front of him to accept donations from the people. the people were passing the streets but hardly someone come to him and offers some bucks in his cap to help him. The was blind but could sense that not many people are willing to help him and was saddened by this. A man passing through the street saw the boy, he read the board and saw the cap which is almost empty except few coins in it. The man walks nearer to the boy takes his board and writes something on another side of the board and asks the boy to hold it in such a way that people could read the new words written by him. The man then put some money in the boy's cap and walk away. After some time many people passing over started putting money in the boy's cap and within an hour the cap was almost filled with money. The man who wrote something on the board again comes to the boy, picks up the cap, and gave it to the blind boy. The boy recognize that he was the same person who wrote on his board and only after which he was being able to get money. The boy humbly asks the man, what he has written on the board. the man answered, "I have not written anything different than what you wrote, I just change the way." the lines written by the man were "It is a very beautiful day, but I can not see it. please help me." This line makes the people understand how lucky they are that they can see this beautiful day, this understanding generates the feeling of gratitude, gratitude toward the almighty, gratitude toward nature for making them self-sufficient. this feeling of gratitude made them help the blind boy and understand his problem.

The feeling of gratitude always keeps us aware about the fortune of things we have. which may be our good health, our family, our friends, food to eat, clothes to wear, and many more. because not everyone in this world is fortunate enough to have all this. This feeling will always help to work hard but with the least and most logical expectations. many times the expectations are very impractical and therefore the least probability of fulfilling them. This leads to unsatisfied life full of complaints. the feeling of gratitude to avoid this and you will experience a stress-free life with positive vibes all around because instead of complaining about what you don't have now you will be thanking and expressing gratitude for what you have.
Practicing to express gratitude will make you and your surroundings

positive and joyful. A very small act of yours can add to this. for example while getting out of your taxi, thanking your driver for making you reach safely and timely, thanking your lift-man, thanking your maid, thanking your subordinates, thanking your watchman, or thanking anyone who you feel has somehow directly or indirectly contributed in your life. Just a simple act of thanking and a smile can make another person's day and even yours also. Because the joy of giving is never less, especially when you are giving your gratitude to someone.

It is simply unbelievable that just an act of practicing gratitude and contributing a lot to your transformation. If you made expressing gratitude a habit, you will definitely find many positive changes in you, such as improved mental state, good sleep at night, improved person-to-person connection, strengthen relationships, good and improved social connect, and many more. I experienced a big transformation in me after I started practicing gratitude. It helped me to reduce friction and heated arguments with anyone. I also started respecting the opinion of another person too and can now have good and outcome-based discussions.

How can we practice expressing gratitude?

As we had already discussed that expressing our gratitude is much more than feeling grateful or being polite to someone. There are a few simple ways you can start with and you be habitual to practice it daily.

Appreciate someone for any nice act:

If you come across someone who did something nice you can simply appreciate him. you can say, "Hey, you have done a great job....," "how kind of you, thank you," or "thank you for being with me." how simple is that, just a few words but these words will do the magic, the magic of transformation. You are getting transformed but at the same time, you are sowing the seeds of transformation in another person too.

Express gratitude through an act of kindness:

just like we came across the story of a blind boy and how people helped him with money once they feel like expressing their gratitude for what they are having. gratitude evolves in you when you recognize that someone has done something good for us, this makes us more conscious and kind. We may work on returning the favor by doing something special for the other person. You may know about "pass it forward", if someone is helping somebody, he may ask that man to help another needy person in return when he will be in a condition to offer help. Just imagine if these wheels keep rolling you will be witnessing kindness and kindness in the air.

At least one thank a day:

simply start with a single thank a day. every day just thinks about what has happened to you during the day, and what are the things that you are grateful for, while thinking, be conscious about your thoughts. You will feel grateful for something or someone which has appealed to you the most. You can sense the emotion within you when you think of it. just express your gratitude for the same and see how better you will feel. Being surrounded by lot many things and many people, you can easily recognize one act to be grateful about. when I was in school, we were taught to express our gratitude before having our tiffins towards the almighty for the food we got. Before every lunch we use to practice it and believe me we always feel positive and enthusiastic after doing it. Probably this was the only thing in my school life that I use to do willingly without the teacher's pressure. small but effective practice to start with.

Observe the beauty in nature:

My favorite practice is observing the beauty in Nature around us. I just love doing this. For practicing this, you don't need to travel to the hill station or any beach or any forest or any garden, you just need to be aware and you will see you are surrounded by the tremendous beauty of nature. What you need to do is to be open and be aware to feel the beauty. The shades of sky, the sound of the wind flowing and gently touching you, the chirping of birds, trees, the fallen brown leaves, flowers, the sun, each day changed shape of the moon, the stars on the wide black canvas of night sky, mind pleasing rains, sound of each water drop, grass on the roadside, the loveable street dogs, cows, and many many more things. My friend took up a similar pastime that had a lovely element to it. He enjoys being outside and taking in the beauty of nature. When he feels like it, he searches for a heart-shaped formation in the nature and takes a photo of it. Heart formations seen in the form of leaves, clouds, stones, petals of flowers, and sticky rainfall, and in many more things. I frequently receive these photos on my phone from him, and I'm always amazed by their beauty.

I started doing this, and over time it evolved into a hobby, then a habit, of noticing the beauty around me and taking pictures of it. My cellphone gallery is nearly full of images of the nature. By doing it, you'll feel better, less stressed, and more motivated. You'll have a sense of appreciation for nature for making our lives so simple just by being there.

# CHAPTER FIVE

# BE FRIEND WITH THE UNCONSCIOUS MIND

Transformation can only happen if it is done with full willingness. This could be possible by building rapport with the unconscious mind. It's simply like your conscious mind is the manager in an office and the unconscious mind is the employees in the office. now what happens many times, the manager wants that the employees should behave in a certain manner, he may instruct the employees to improve their productivity, to work after office hours, to maintain decorum in the office, to achieve the set target, or anything else. But it often seems that the employees ignore the manager or even go out of their way to do the opposite of what's being instructed to them. we always think to transform ourselves and wanted to incline ourselves toward the positive side. we always decide to change like, " I will start exercising daily," "I will stop rash driving hereafter," "I will quit smoking," or "I will more humble while interacting from now onwards." But, most of the time we fail to do these. To understand the way that most of us relate to the unconscious, we will go through an example. Someone who has decided to stop eating junk food and sweets will by chance eat it. He starts hammering himself, "what a fool I am," "How I can lose my control?" "Ohh... I don't have strong willpower," "I am not a firm decision maker," and many more such slaps. Just like this incident, just think some another person is continuously instructing you don't eat junk food and sweets, but by any chance, you failed to do so and the person starts verbally abusing you again and again for your act. Would you feel like maintaining any relations with the person? This is what most of us are doing with our unconscious mind, the rapport with the unconscious mind gets disturbed. To avoid this, we should be more practical and logical while giving instructions to the unconscious mind and treat it with respect.

Now, the important task is to how we could work with the unconscious mind so that IT can be easy to deal with the conscious and unconscious mind. For this, we need to know that our both minds are very different and work in very different ways from each other. If we are planning to execute any act, it is done by the conscious mind. Whereas, while doing it, if we get feelings of enthusiasm, nervousness, or excitement, it is with the unconscious mind. Our conscious mind has limitations to only focus on the activities that we are doing at that time instance, but at the same time, the unconscious mind pays attention to many other things simultaneously. The unconscious mind is just like a wide-angle camera lens with a broad focus, and the conscious mind is just like a portrait camera lens which focuses on the object and blurs other things. The conscious mind is more practical and logical, but the unconscious mind works on intuition or feelings and has a huge storage of our memories. The conscious mind is just like a manager and the unconscious mind is just like the employee who obeys him.

To make the conscious and unconscious mind work together, what is to be done is that the manager should perfectly plan the tasks and convey them to the employees clearly and respectfully. The employees do need to listen to the instructions carefully and start working accordingly. If however, the employees don't listen carefully to their manager, the organization will suffer a lot. Adding to this, if the manager doesn't flow any instructions and lets the employees do whatever they wish, then obviously the organization will collapse completely. Just like this, many people fail to understand the relation between the conscious and the unconscious mind, and as a result, suffer a lot or even collapse completely. This is only because they are not in rapport with the unconscious mind. They don't give instructions specifically and clearly and also don't listen to the voice of the unconscious mind.

The unconscious mind is a powerful force that plays a significant role in shaping our thoughts, behaviors, and emotions. It is the part of the mind that is responsible for processing information and experiences that are not currently in our conscious awareness. Many people believe that the unconscious mind is a mysterious and unfathomable entity, but in reality, it is something that we can learn to understand and work with. Some of the things which we can do are,

Practicing Mindfulness: It is a powerful way to build a rapport with the unconscious mind. You can do some easy activities to connect with your unconscious mind. Find a quiet and comfortable place where you can be without being disturbed. This helps to focus on the present moment. Later on, begin with focusing attention on your breath. Try to experience the breath moving in and moving out. Breathe deeply and slowly. As you focus on your breath, you will come across a lot of many thoughts flowing randomly When this happens, simply notice the thoughts that are arising in your mind. Don't try to neglect them or even don't get involved in them, simply observe them. If your mind begins to run, gently bring your attention back to your breath. Just be calm and be aware of your thoughts for several minutes. You can start with five minutes and gradually increase the time as you become more comfortable with the practice. After some time, try to expand your awareness to include your body and your surroundings. Repeat this regularly. Mindfulness is a skill that needs to be practiced regularly. Try to practice mindfulness every day, even if it's just for a few minutes.

By practicing mindfulness, you can learn to observe your thoughts and emotions without getting caught up in them. This can help you to understand how your unconscious mind is influencing your behavior and make conscious choices about how you respond to different situations.

Examine Yourself: Take the time to explore your ideas and feelings, as well as the patterns that determine your behaviour. You may learn more about your subconscious mind by investigating yourself. The unconscious is the brain's largest and deepest component, holding our most private thoughts, feelings, and wants. Reflecting on your experiences and emotions aids in the clarification of your subconscious mind and the better understanding of your aims. You can become more mindful through self-reflection and introspection. Examining your ideas and feelings allows you to identify areas that require change and learning, as well as build methods to address them. You may strengthen your relationship with yourself by working with your subconscious mind. This can enhance your mental and emotional wellness as well as your self-esteem. You can start doing these by practicing journaling. You will come across the detailing of this practice in the chapter on journaling.

Just Visualize: Visualization is the process of creating mental images of the things you want to achieve or experience. By visualizing your goals and desires, you can help align your unconscious mind with your conscious intentions. This can be an effective way to overcome limiting beliefs and negative thought patterns that are holding you back.

Mediation: Meditation is a practice that helps you to focus your mind and become more aware of your thoughts, feelings, and physical sensations. It can help you to relax and quiet your mind, making it easier to access the unconscious mind.

Read and Learn: Reading books and articles about the unconscious mind can help you to gain a deeper understanding of how it works and how it influences your thoughts and behaviors.

Positive Affirmations: Positive affirmations are statements that you repeat to yourself to help change negative thoughts and beliefs. By repeating positive affirmations, you can help to reprogram your unconscious mind and align it with your conscious goals and intentions.

You need to remember that befriending the unconscious mind is a process and it takes time and practice. By incorporating these tips and activities into your daily routine, you can gradually develop a deeper understanding of your unconscious mind and learn to work with it more effectively.

# Understanding and Utilizing your Strengths and Weaknesses

Understanding your Strengths and Weaknesses and Utilizing them is an important aspect of personal development. It includes identifying and evaluating the skills, qualities, and abilities that you have in you, as well as the things where you have scope for improvement. By understanding your strengths and weaknesses, you can make more informed decisions and take action toward your goals.

A personal SWOT analysis is an extremely useful tool for self-transformation by providing a clear view of your current situation. It enables you to identify your strengths and weaknesses, along with it the opportunities and threats that you may face in your life. By knowing your current situation, you can make wise decisions and take action for moving toward your goals. It is useful for self-transformation because it helps you to identify areas of improvement. By identifying your weaknesses, you can focus on developing your skills and knowledge in those areas, which can help you become more confident, capable, and effective.

The self-transformation can be boost up by identifing the opportunities for growth. By identifying your strengths, you can focus on building on them, and by identifying opportunities in your personal and professional life, you can make the most of them. For example, if your goal is to advance in your career, you might focus on developing your professional skills and networking to take advantage of job opportunities. A personal SWOT analysis can also be used to identify and address any potential roadblocks or obstacles that may be preventing you from achieving your goals. By identifying your weaknesses and potential threats, you can take steps to mitigate them and reduce their impact on your progress.

Using this tool, you can establish a sense of self-awareness, which is an important step in self-transformation. It helps you understand your own thoughts process and behaviors, and how they may impact your ability to achieve your goals. It can also help you identify any fear or habits that may resist you to transform.

Here are the steps to do a SWOT analysis of yourself:

- Know your strengths: Here strength refer to the things that you do well, the qualities and habits that makes you quit ahead of others, and the things that you are more confident about. For example, your strength may be being a good speaker, being confident, having strong moral values, or being a skilled person in any activity.
- Know your weakness: Weaknesses are the areas where you are lacking and have a scope for improvement, you can also address the things which you feel are challenging for you. Examples of weaknesses might include being shy, having poor time management habits, low willpower, or being less confident.
- Know your opportunities: Opportunities are the factors that could set a path for you toward your goals or improve your situation. Examples of opportunities might include a new job opportunity, Transfer to a new city, a course or training program, or a business opportunity that could benefit your business.
- Know your threats: The things that could have a negative impact on your life or act as obstacles in the path of your goal can be treated as threats. Just like negative market situations, Politics in the workplace, or your competitor.
- Analyze your SWOT: Once you are aware of your strengths, weaknesses, opportunities, and threats, you will understand how they relate to each other and your goals. For example, you can use your strengths to take advantage of any opportunity, or you can use your weaknesses to identify areas where you need to improve. Even you can use your strength to overshadow any weakness.
- Make an action plan: Once the analysis is done, you can create an action plan to use the opportunities in a better way and work on your weaknesses for further improvement. The plan may have, working on specific goals, scheduling for improvement, or undertaking pieces of training.

You should do such analysis periodically. As you move forward in your life and your goals change, it is important to reevaluate your strengths, weaknesses, opportunities, and threats to see if they have changed.

Carring out your self analysis can play a crucial role in personal development. Here are a few ways that it can help:

Makes you more confident: Once you know your strengths, your confidence gets boosted along with it. Our skills and abilities make you more confident in your actions, which can lead to greater success in your life.

Setting realistic targets: Once you understand your strengths and weaknesses, you will be able to know your abilities and points of you and at the same time you know where you lack. These help you in setting realistic goals which will be achievable for you. And you can avoid setting goals that are out of reach, these make you focus on things that you are good at and set realistic targets that you can achieve.

More self-awareness: Knowing your strengths and weaknesses makes you more self-aware. Self-awareness acts as fuel for self-transformation, these can lead to better decision-making, improved relationships, and a greater sense of personal control over your life.

Know where you stand: By understanding your weaknesses, you can know your current situation and come across the fact that where you stand. This makes you identify areas where improvement is needed. You can focus on developing new skills or knowledge.

Channeling your time and energy: By understanding your strengths and weaknesses, you can better prioritize your time and energy. You can focus on the things that you are good at and enjoy, and avoid wasting time and energy on things that you struggle with.

# SWOT

## Strengths

Things that you do well, the qualities and habits that makes you quit ahead of others, and the things that you are more confident about.

## Weaknesses

Areas where you are lacking and have a scope for improvement, you can also address the things which you feel are challenging for you.

## Opportunities

Factors that could set a path for you toward your goals or improve your situation.

.

## Threats

Things that could have a negative impact on your life or act as obstacles in the path of your goal

Template for SWOT

CHAPTER SEVEN

# Go for Continuous Improvement

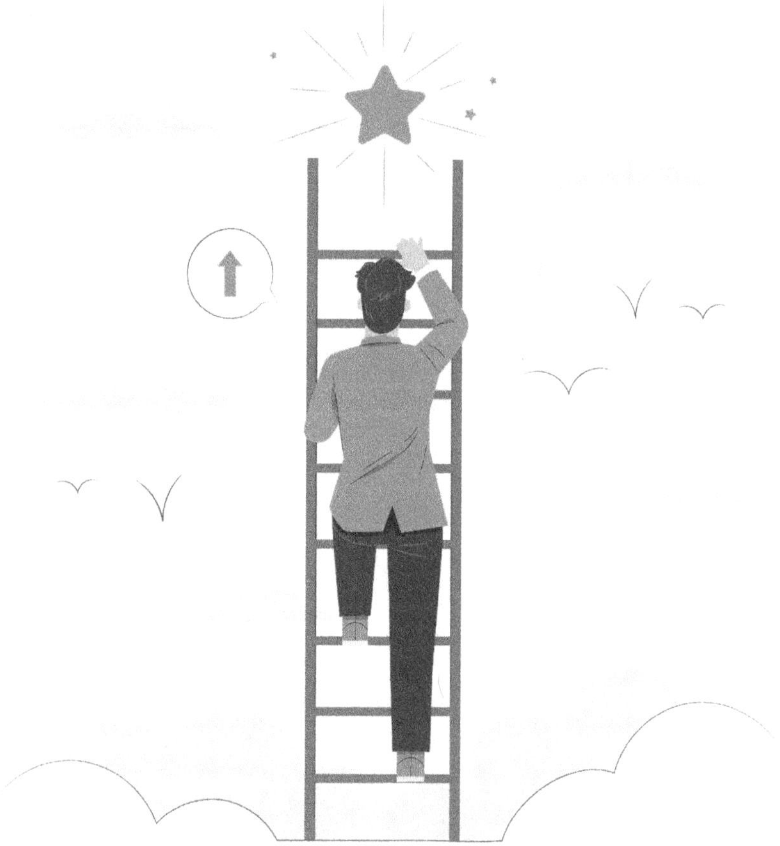

Self-transformation is a journey that requires constant effort, dedication, and a willingness to improve. Continuous improvement is one of the essential components for achieving this. Continuous improvement is the process of always aiming to improve oneself, one's actions, and one's progress. It's a way of thinking that keeps us inspired, concentrated, and flexible. We can all improve ourselves, but it can be difficult to know where to begin. The Japanese concept of "continuous improvement" may be useful in this situation. It is a technique for implementing small and incremental changes continuously for betterment. Although the idea is used in various industries, we can also use it to gradually better ourselves. We can accomplish our objectives and enhance our general well-being by applying the concept to self-transformation.

Self-transformation requires constant improvement because it keeps people motivated and focused. When you see growth and improvement, it can inspire you to keep going for your objectives. Furthermore, being able to track our development and see the fruits of our efforts can help you to maintain your focus and dedication to the transformation process. When you accomplish our goals, it gives a sense of accomplishment and keeps you on track. The fact that constant development fosters your capacity for resilience and adaptability is another crucial element for self-transformation. You may make sure we are prepared to respond to new situations and problems by always seeking methods to do better. This can make you stronger and more equipped to face challenges that may come up throughout the transformation process. It makes you more resilient in the face of change and more equipped to handle whatever life throws to you.

Continuous improvement also aids in the establishment of a growth mentality. It is more likely to see problems and hurdles as chances for development and learning when you approach them with an attitude of constant improvement. This can assist you in acquiring the knowledge and attitude required to accomplish the objectives and gradually moves towards betterment. When you have a growth mindset, you view obstacles as chances to learn and develop, which helps to improve as people.

You can follow the stages for implementing Continuous improvement;

1. Set a goal
2. Break down the goal into small steps
3. Take action
4. Measure progress
5. Reflect and adjust
6. Repeat
7. Witness your achievements

Setting a goal is the first step in using continuous improvement for self-transformation. It might concern the relationships, careers, health, or any other area of your life. You can establish a specific, measurable, achievable, relevant, and time-bound (SMART) goal after identifying an area that needs improvement.

The next step after establishing a goal is to divide it into small steps. For example, if you want to lose 10 kg in the next two months, starting with healthier eating and more exercise could be the first step. This increases the goal's reachability and speeds up its accomplishment. It is essential to take these small steps. Just like, if our first goal is to eat healthier, you can begin by making minor adjustments in the diet, like avoiding junk foods or limiting our portion sizes. By doing this, you can gradually form healthy habits that become a part of the daily routine.

Regularly tracking progress is another important point of continuous improvement. This can assists in monitoring the progress and locating areas that require improvement. For instance, weighing yourself every week and record your progress as the objective is to lose weight. Reflecting and changing the plan as necessary is another important step. It might be necessary to modify the plan or adopt a different strategy if the progress is slower than what was thought. Just like, you may need to change your diet or exercise routine if you discover that you are not losing weight as quickly as you had hoped.

You can accomplish your goals and gradually get better by repeating this process of deciding on small steps, taking action, monitoring your progress, reflecting, and making adjustments. Additionally, it is important to recognize your accomplishments along the way and your progress.

Continuous improvement takes time but comes out with results and is easy to implement as it is needed to do it bit by bit. There is a live example in which I have witnessed the transformation through Continuous improvement. One of my colleagues had the sufficient technical expertise and was well-liked in the institute for his active participation. But he often felt that his ability to speak English well was missing. He was conscious of his shortcomings and was having strong willpower to improve them.

But since learning a language is never simple, he began by taking small steps.He began reading books in English, using the dictionary to expand his vocabulary, speaking to students and colleagues in English, and taking many other similar actions. I was pleased but also surprised to observe the shift as I saw him make progress and gain more self-assurance. I saw his dedication when he and I met at the train station at the same time while we were both waiting for the train. I observed him watching at the screen of his smartphone while wearing headphones. I found him watching a Bollywood film with dubbed English audio and subtitles when I went to see him.He was so into it that he even don't recognize me for a time. He was making every effort to carry out his plan for continued progress, and he was even making use of the waiting period to get one step closer to his objective. When I communicated with him about his transformation journey, he told me how step by step he did the things and how he used his interest in watching movies for achieving his goal. He use to take regular feedback from friends about his way of communication and was also solving online tests of English for self-assessment. He now has a strong speaking voice and a solid mastery of the English language. I have listened to his lectures and workshops and have been motivated to improve myself.

# Identifying the Root Causes

One way to identify the root cause of a problem is to use a method called "root cause analysis." This is a process of identifying the underlying causes of a problem, rather than just treating the symptoms.

**"5 Whys"** is a simple and effective tool for identifying the underlying causes of a problem. It involves asking "why" a problem is occurring, and then continuing to ask "why" to each answer until the root cause is identified.

For example, if a problem is that a there is no output on computer, the "5 Whys" process might involve asking the following questions:

*"**Why** is there is no output on computer?*
*Answer: The computer is not working"*

*"**Why** is the computer is not working?*
*Answer: There is no power to the computer"*

*"**Why** is there no power to the computer?*
*Answer: The power cord is disconnected"*

*"**Why** is the power cord disconnected?*
*Answer: The operator unplugged it"*

*"**Why** did the operator unplug it?*
*Answer: To clean the area and forgot to plug it back in"*

By using this method, the root cause of the problem (operator forgetting to plug in the power cord) is identified and can be addressed.

This is just an easy example. By practicing it for any problem of day-to-day life you could reach the root cause of that problem. This can be used for simple problems, whereas the bigger problem with too many causes can be addressed by the cause-and-effect diagram.

### Cause-and-effect diagram

The very supportive concept to the 80/20 rule is the fishbone diagram also known as Ishikawa diagram, or cause-and-effect diagram, is a tool used to identify the root cause of a problem. It is a visual representation of the possible causes of a problem and is often used in quality control and process improvement. The Ishikawa diagram is an important tool in self-transformation process as it helps individuals to identify the root cause of their problems which can be related to internal and external factors. By doing so, individuals can work on the root cause of the problem and not just the symptoms, which leads to a more effective and long-term solution. It also helps to understand the relationship between different factors and how they contribute to the problem, which is essential in developing effective solutions. This process of identifying the problem and finding solutions, also helps in building self-awareness and self-motivation, which are key aspects of self-transformation.

Here is a step-by-step guide on how to use an cause-and-effect diagram for day-to-day problems:

Step 1: Identify the problem: Clearly define the problem you are trying to solve. For example, "I am having trouble falling asleep at night."

Step 2: Create the diagram: Draw the "spine" of the fishbone diagram, which is a line that represents the problem. Then, draw lines coming off the spine to create the "bones" of the fish, which represent the different categories of causes. Common categories include people, equipment, materials, methods, and environment.

Step 3: Identify the causes: For each category, brainstorm and list all the possible causes of the problem. For example, under the category of "people," causes could include stress, anxiety, and poor sleep habits.

Step 4: Organize the causes: Group the causes together based on their similarities and relationships. For example, "stress" and "anxiety" could be grouped together under the category of "emotional causes."

Step 5: Analyze the data: Look for patterns and connections between the causes. Identify the most likely causes of the problem and those that have the greatest impact.

Step 6: Develop solutions: Use the information gathered in the Ishikawa diagram to develop solutions to the problem. For example, if stress and anxiety were identified as the main causes of trouble sleeping, a solution could be to implement stress management techniques or seek therapy.

Seeing the fishbone diagram process for ' sleeping problem' in deatils:

The Ishikawa diagram for "I am having trouble falling asleep at night" would look something like this:

The spine of the fishbone diagram would be the statement "I am having trouble falling asleep at night"

The bones of the fish would represent the different categories of causes. The categories could include:

People (e.g. psychological factors, poor sleep habits)

Environment (e.g. noise, light, temperature, bed comfort)

Medical (e.g. health conditions, medications)

Lifestyle (e.g. diet, exercise, caffeine, alcohol)

Social (e.g. More social life, stress, anxiety, relationship issues)

Under each category, there would be specific causes listed. For example, under the category of "People" there could be:

Psychological factors (e.g. stress, anxiety, depression)

Poor sleep habits (e.g. irregular sleep schedule, using electronic devices before bed)

Under the category of "Environment", there could be:

Noise (e.g. traffic, neighbors)

Light (e.g. street lights, electronic devices)

Temperature (e.g. too hot or too cold)

Bed comfort (e.g. mattress, pillows, sheets)

And so on for the other categories.

Once all the causes are listed, it would be possible to group them together based on their similarities and relationships. Finally, by analyzing the data, one can identify the most likely causes of the problem and those that have the greatest impact, and use this information to develop solutions to improve sleep.

It's worth to mention that this Ishikawa diagram is just an example and it can be adjusted according to the specific situation.

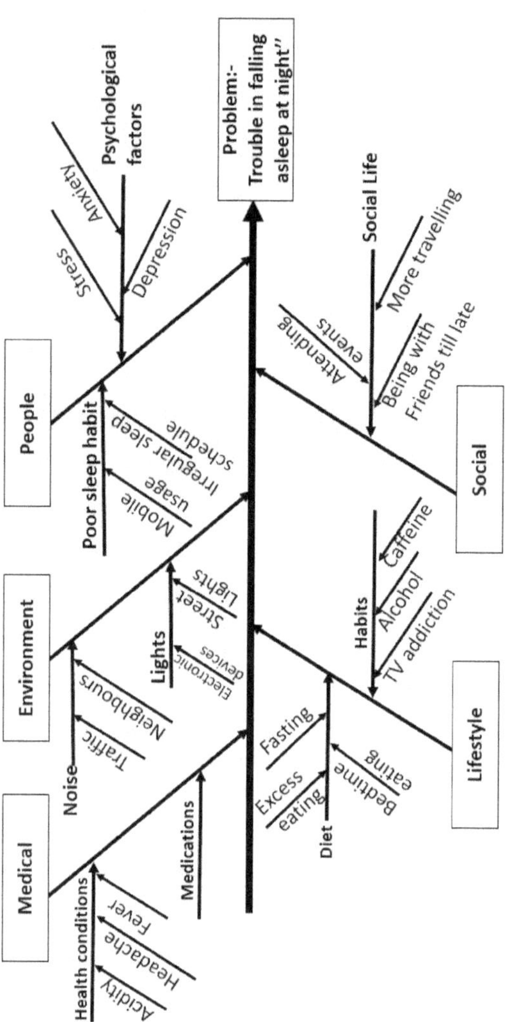



Example of Cause and Effect diagram for trouble in falling asleep at night

# CHAPTER NINE

# KNOW THE '80/20' CONCEPT

The 80/20 rule, is often used as a tool of management which states that 80% of effects come from 20% of causes. In general, this rule is applied to many areas of industries and management, but here we will understand the rule and let us see its usage in our life to ease the transformation. Many times when we think of changing something to resolve any problem in our life, we always wonder, "from where I should start?", "There are so many problems in my life, how to resolve them all?", "Out of so many problems, how can I decide which should be targeted first?". The 80/20 rule will come out with answers to all these questions. Here we will see the process of using this powerful tool to identify and address the underlying causes of your problems. By focusing on the key areas that are responsible for most of your results, you can improve your overall well-being and effectiveness. It is important to remember that this is an ongoing process and that the key is to continuously track and measure your progress. When it is about solving problems in our lives, we often focus on the symptoms rather than the root cause. Neglecting the root cause of any problem, will not make you to reach to the solution of the problem. By applying the 80/20 rule, we can concentrate to identify and address the underlying causes of all our problems. Just like, if you're facing poblem of stress and anxiety, you may find that 80% of your stress is coming from 20% of the things in your life. By identifying and addressing these specific causes of stress, you can make a significant impact on your overall well-being. As the rule, states that 80% of effects come from 20% of causes. This principle can be applied to many areas of life, including problem-solving, time management, and productivity. The basics behind the rule is that a small number of causes can have a excessive effect on the outcome.

To apply the 80/20 rule in your life, it is important to take a step back and take a look at the bigger picture. you need to identify the areas where you are struggling and then try to find the root causes. Once the identification is done, you can then start addressing them and making the necessary changes. It is important to keep in mind that the ratio of it may not be always 80/20 and may vary depending on the scenario. The key is to identify the key areas that need to be focused on and make the necessary changes.

The rule can be also applied to focus on the 20% of activities that are giving you the most results. By focusing on the things that are working well, you can achieve more with less effort. Many times all goes well in your life, but you are not been able to keep it going. Because you may not know the reason behind the good things happening to you. You may use this tool to identify those activities responsible for great things happening to you. You may find that you are spending a lot of time on activities that don't bring much value to your life, while a small number of activities are responsible for most of your personal growth. By identifying and focusing on these key activities, you can improve your overall well-being and effectiveness. Tracking and measuring your progress by using the rule can be helpful to identify the areas that are working well and the areas that are needed to be improvement. This will help you to make better decisions about where to focus your time and energy. The 80/20 rule is not a one-time fix, it's a continuous process. As you go on to make changes and achieve your goals, new problems and challenges will arise. By continuing to apply this rule, you can continue to identify and address the causes of your problems and maintain a sense of balance and harmony in your life.

The 80/20 rule can also be applied to time management. By identifying and focusing on the most important tasks, you can be more productive and make better use of your time. The idea is that 20% of your activities will lead to 80% of your results, while the other 80% of your activities will lead to only 20% of your results. An example of this in time management would be that 20% of the tasks on your to-do list are likely to be the most important and will have the greatest impact on your goals, while the other 80% may be less important or less urgent. By focusing on 20% of the most important tasks, you can achieve more with your time and make the most progress toward your goals.

The 80/20 rule can also be used way to take a look at your relationships, you may find that a small number of people are responsible for most of the positive or negative experiences in your life. For example, a small number of friends or family members may be responsible for the good experiences in your life. Conversely, a small number of enemies or people around you may be responsible for most of the negative experiences in your life, such as stress, anxiety, and conflict. The rule will make you aware of identifying those persons around you so that you can be with those making you feel good and avoid or be aware of the people who brings stress and problems in your life. By identifying these key relationships, you can make conscious decisions about how to interact with them, and how to invest your time and energy in these relationships.

To understand the implementation of the rule let us see an example of stress management. Here it means that 80% of your stress is coming from 20% of the things causing it. To apply the rule for stress management, you may follow the steps:

Identifying the causes of stress: Try to make a list of everything which may cause stress to you. This may include friends, office work, family, relationships, health, finances, etc. You can use techniques for finding root causes, such as cause and effect diagrams.

Arrange the sources as per priority: Simply check out the list of the causes and rate each cause of stress on a scale of 1 to 10, with 1 as the least stressful and 10 as the most stressful. It will help you to prioritize the causes of stress that are affecting you the most.

Concentrate on the top 20% of causes: Once you come out with your sources of stress and arrange them as per the scale, concentrate on the top 20% of the causes on your list that are causing the most stress. These are the things that you need to work on first.

Plan to reduce or eliminate stress: For each of the stress sources from the 20% list, think about what is to be done to reduce or eliminate them. This could include delegating work in the office, improving communication in relationships, managing the finances effectively, or working for good health for stress.

Implementing the plan: Once you have come out with the plans, it's time to put them into action. Start with the most significant sources of stress and work your way down the list.

By doing these you can focus on the top 20% of stress sources, and then you can have a big impact on reducing your overall stress levels. you should be aware of the fact that like other strategies of transformation, it is also a continual process, so be sure to regularly reassess your causes and adjust your strategies as needed.

Here you can see the simplest way of doing the practical implementation of the concept to the day-to-day life problem. Here from the below chart, it can be clearly seen that out of nine causes of stress majorly only two are having a majority of the impact. Thus, focusing on only these two causes there will be a big impact on reducing the overall stress.

| Causes for Stress to me | Scale from 1 to 10 | | | | | | | | | |
|---|---|---|---|---|---|---|---|---|---|---|
| | 1 | 2 | 3 | 4 | 5 | 6 | 7 | 8 | 9 | 10 |
| 1. Work pressure | ① | ② | ③ | | | | | | | |
| 2. Friends | ① | | | | | | | | | |
| 3. Unorganised work | ① | ② | ③ | | | | | | | |
| 4. Relationships | ① | | | | | | | | | |
| 5. Conflicts at workplace | ① | ② | ③ | ④ | ⑤ | | | | | |
| 6. Finances | ① | ② | ③ | | | | | | | |
| 7. Being too busy | ① | ② | ③ | ④ | ⑤ | ⑥ | ⑦ | ⑧ | | |
| 8. Family | ① | | | | | | | | | |
| 9. Unhealthy lifestyle | ① | ② | ③ | ④ | ⑤ | ⑥ | ⑦ | ⑧ | ⑨ | |

Example of implementing the concept to the stress problem

# CHAPTER TEN

# THE TRANSFORMATIVE '5S'

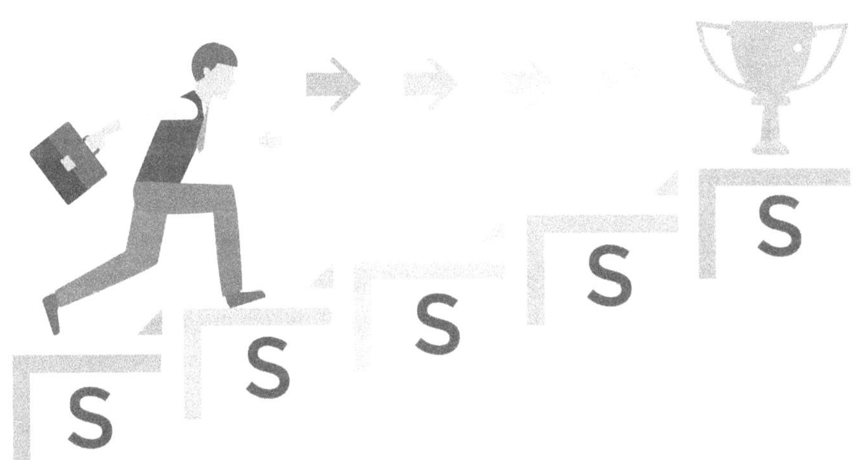

Just like the 80/20 concept and Ishikawa diagram, "5S" is also a lean tool used in many industries for years for identifying the problems in companies and eliminating them. Here we will give a try of applying the '5S' for self-transformation. The concept of '5S' is a Japanese philosophy that refers to five steps for organizing and improving the efficiency of a workplace. The '5S' means the five Japanese words, they are Seiri, Seiton, Seiso, Seiketsu, and Shitsuke. These means Sort, Set in order, Sweep, Standardize, and Sustain. Further, we will see how it can also be applied to personal development to help individuals become more organized and improve their quality of life.

---

## *Sort----Set in order----Sweep----Standardize----Sustain.*

---

**Sort:** The 5S methodology is a widely recognized and widely used organizational method in various industries. However, in the context of self-transformation, the first step of 5S, sorting has a deeper meaning. Sorting through your thoughts, values, and habits is a critical aspect of personal growth. This step involves introspection and self-reflection to identify what is important and what is not in your life. The goal of this step is to eliminate anything that is not aligned with personal growth and to create a roadmap for positive change. For example, someone who struggles with managing time may identify that they have difficulty prioritizing tasks. By observing their behaviors, they can understand the underlying reasons for these problems and develop a plan to overcome them. This may involve setting specific goals, creating a daily routine, or finding more effective time management techniques.

This first step in the 5S methodology for self-transformation provides the foundation for positive change and personal growth by helping individuals to identify and eliminate negative patterns and to focus on what is truly important.

---

**Set in order:** The second step in the 5S methodology for self-transformation is a simplification or set in order. This step involves reducing distractions, removing unnecessary items from both physical and mental spaces, and focusing on what is truly important in your life. The goal is to set the important things in order for eliminating excess and keep only what is necessary. This saves time and energy and focuses on what is truly important.

Set in order can be applied to various aspects of one's life, such as their schedule, habits, and possessions. For example, someone may simplify their daily routine by prioritizing tasks, reducing social media use, and setting clear boundaries for work and personal time. By doing so, they can ensure that they have enough time and energy to focus on what is truly important to them, such as self-care or personal growth.

Additionally, simplification also involves reducing distractions in one's physical and mental spaces and helps in properly organizing thoughts and tasks which can have a positive impact on mental health.

––––––

**Sweep:** Sweep is the third step in the 5S method for self-transformation. This step includes pushing out the negative thoughts, feelings, and behaviors that are limiting your transformation. The purpose of this step is to establish a clean and healthy mental and emotional environment, which is necessary for growth and satisfaction. Sweep requires individuals to take an active role in managing their thoughts and emotions. This involves reframing negative thoughts into positive ones and engaging in activities that promote mental and emotional health. For example, someone who struggles with anxiety may practice mindfulness, journaling, or talk to a trusted friend or therapist to help sweep away negative thoughts. Sweep also involves cleaning up one's physical and mental space. This is just like removing unnecessary items from one's home, cleaning their work area, and throwing the unnecessary things. By doing so, individuals can create a more positive and organized environment, which can help them feel refreshed and motivated.

It is important to note that sweeping is not simply about sweeping away negative thoughts, emotions, and behaviors. It is also about creating a positive and supportive environment that promotes growth. This may involve creating routines, setting goals, and surrounding oneself with positive and supportive people.

––––––

**Standardize:** Standardizeis the fourth step in the 5S method for self-transformation. This step involves building beneficial habits, behaviors, and routines to provide a sense of structure and stability in your life. This step's purpose is to increase consistency. Set specific goals and stick to them consistently to standardize positive habits, behaviors, and routines.

This helps in developing routines and procedures that support your aim and make it easier to keep your life in order. For example, someone may set aside time each day for exercise and make it a mandatory component of their daily routine. This helps in the development of a consistent and structured routine, which can promote health.

Here, you should also establish standards for organizing and maintaining order in your life. This may include creating a daily schedule, setting priorities, and establishing habits. For example, You can simply standardize your morning routine by setting a fixed wake-up time, morning exercise, and having a healthy breakfast every day. This helps to create a sense of structure and stability in their daily routine. It is important to note that standardizing positive habits, behaviors, and routines requires self-discipline and consistent effort. Individuals must be intentional about sticking to their routines and habits, and be willing to make changes when necessary.

---

**Sustain:** The fifth and final step in the 5S methodology for self-transformation is sustain. This step is about maintaining and sustaining the positive changes and habits that have been developed in the previous steps. The goal of this step is to ensure continued success and progress towards personal growth and development. To sustain positive changes, you must engage in ongoing self-reflection, goal setting, and regular practice of the habits and routines established in the previous steps. This requires discipline, effort, and a commitment to personal growth. For example, someone may sustain their positive habits by setting regular check-ins with themselves and tracking their progress towards their goals. This helps to keep them motivated and on track towards their desired outcome.

In this step, you should also continually monitor and adjust your habits and routines to ensure continued success. This means regularly reviewing your progress and making changes as needed to keep moving forward. For example, someone may adjust their exercise routine if they find that it is no longer working for them, or add new habits to their daily routine if they feel like they are not making progress towards their goals. It is important to understand that sustaining positive changes is a continuous process. You must be willing to adapt and make changes as necessary, while also celebrating their progress and successes along the way.

# CHAPTER ELEVEN

# The Art of Decision Making

Decision making is an essential part of self-transformation because it gives you the power to take charge of your life and mould it in line with your values and objectives. Every day we take a lot of many decisions, some small and some big. Small decisions such as choosing clothes, choosing from the restaurant menu, choosing the mode of transport, and many more, and big decisions such as choosing a career, switching the job, getting married, and many more. Sometimes it is difficult to decide which one is the best. However, it is important to remember that every selection we make, even the smaller ones, can have a substantial result on our lives. It is essential to make the right choices, those that match our values and aspirations so that we can move towards a more successful and satisfying life. One method to make sure that we are making the right decision is to take the time to appraise the options and contemplate the expected outcomes of each. Additionally, it is important to seek advice from people we trust, such as family and friends, or even experts. They can provide an alternate outlook and help us recognize things we may have overlooked. Another way to pick the correct choice is to listen to our intuition, that internal voice that guides us. It may not always be the easiest or most popular option, but it is usually the one that is authentic to our identity and what we believe in.

Being mindful and logical while making choices will help you create the life as per your desire. It also enhances your understanding of yourself, including your thinking process, beliefs, and any elements that could influence your decision. Making thoughtful selections enables you to grow personally by learning from your mistakes. It also boosts your self-confidence and self-esteem as you begin to believe in your capacity to make the correct choices. On the contrary, hasty and careless decisions lead to feelings of being trapped, regret, and dissatisfaction.Taking the time to view your goals, values, and priorities will help you to choose in line with where you are and where you want to be in life.

In order to make good decisions, it is important to understand our own thought process, values and biases that may affect our decision making. This is where self-awareness comes in. By gaining a deeper understanding of ourselves, we can make better decisions.

These have helped me a lot in taking some important decisions in my life. After completing my master's in Engineering, I started working in an automobile company in the project department. The job profile was very good still I was feeling like missing something in life, and was not much happy to be there. To seek answers to these questions, I started monitoring my thought process and values. These help me in understanding myself better and I came across the fact that my priority was my family, my time to explore my interests and hobbies, and along with it my inclination toward the teaching profession. As I was convinced about this 'me', I quit the company job and joined a college as a professor in my hometown. I came crossed the valley of the crucial decision-making process just by understanding my thinking pattern, my values, and my priorities. I am glad that I was able to take that decision and attain my priorities.

Making the appropriate option requires taking into account a number of significant factors while making decisions. The factors such as;

Evaluating the options: One of the important steps in decision-making is to consider all of the options to you and not eliminate any option without evaluating it. You should see the positive and negative points of each option and evaluate the potential consequences of each choice. For example, you have two colleges where you can get admission and you must select one of the two colleges. You're thinking about which college you should attend. One college has a better reputation and offers more facilities to you, even if the other is closer to home and has a lower tuition rate. In this situation, you should examine the benefits and drawbacks of each college and consider the possible effects of your decision. To decide which option is ideal for you, think about the fees, location, reputation, academics, and placement ooportunities.

Seeking advice: To take a wise decision, seeking the advice and guidance of trusted friends, family, and professionals is important. These can help you see things that you might have missed. You're thinking whether to leave your current position or launch your own firm. You're considering creating your own company, but you're unsure if it's the best move. You should in this situation seek the counsel and direction of reliable family members, friends, and experts. The benefits and hazards of starting your own business can be better understood by speaking with a business mentor and financial advisor. I had personally faced this situation in the near past and seeking advice from my family and mentors helped me a lot.

Listen your intuition: Many times, you attempt to decide whether to go for something or not, so pay attention to your gut feeling. Although you're unsure about the best option and have second thoughts. You need to listen to your instincts in such a situation. Even if it is not the most popular or straightforward option, this inner voice might help you make the right choice.

Understand the priorities: Understanding your priorities are most important to you and should be considered when making any decision. You should have a clear understanding of your values and priorities. You should consider which option goes correct with your values and by which option you will attain your priorities.

Think about long-term impact: Considering the long-term: It's crucial to think about how your choice will affect you. Sometimes a quick profit could be attractive, it's important to think about the long-term effects on your life.

For example, if you are considering a move to another city, it's important to consider the long-term impact on your career and your relationships before making a decision.

Be flexible: These qualities are important while making decisions. It's critical to be open to fresh perspectives and options, as well as to be flexible to adjust your thinking about the option so that more knowledge becomes available. For instance, it's crucial to be open to new chances and willing to alter your plan if market conditions change if you're thinking about making a new investment.

Many times the decisions go wrong. There might be many reasons behind the failure. Instead of seeking those reasons and trying to correct the mistakes, it is a general tendency to blame others or the situation for the failure. This thinking will never take you on the right path again. If in case any decision goes wrong, the consequences may be small or big, depending on the situation. Here are some steps you can take to correct the consequences of a wrong decision:

Watch the situation: Watching the situation and understanding the nature of the problem is very important. This helps you in knowing the root cause of the issue and the way to seek a solution for the problem.

Take responsibility: Whenever anything goes wrong in life we always start blaming others for that act. It is important to take responsibility for decisions without any hesitation. This can help in learning from your mistakes and thus will make you take better decisions in the future.

Make and implement the plan: Try to make a plan for addressing the impact of your decision. Make sure that the plan should be time-bound. Once it is done, go for implementing it to correct the mistakes made.

Learn from mistake: Consider the circumstances and your error, then grow from it. Think on what you could have done better and how you may prevent yourself from making the same error in the future.

Keep a positive attitude: In any situation, it's important to keep a positive attitude and not to let the consequences of a bad decision define you. Learn from the experience and move forward.

# THE 'P-D-C-A' PATH TO PERSONAL DEVELOPMENT

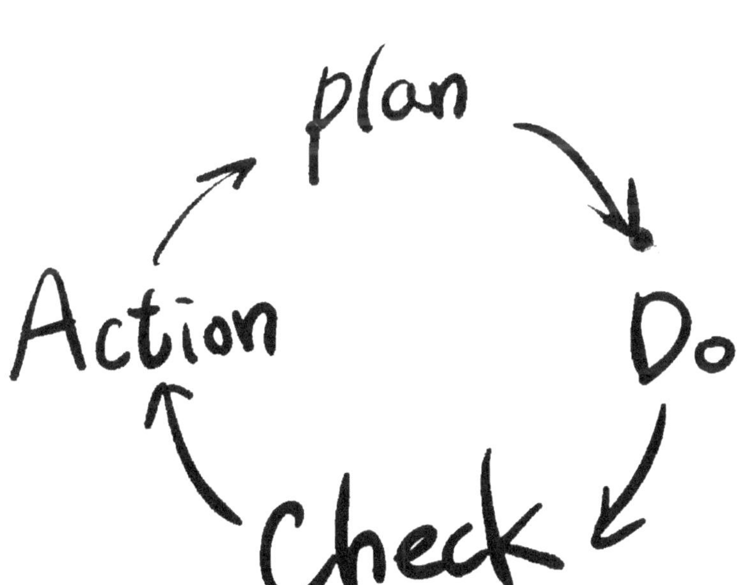

The PDCA (Plan-Do-Check-Act) cycle is a four-step model for improvement and assessment and is used in businesses and organizations. It is helpful to identify a problem or opportunity and determine a plan to address it. Then take action, check the results and make necessary adjustments and improvements to the plan and repeat the cycle. This framework can be applied for self-transformation as well.

———

**Plan:** Plan: This step includes identifying your present personality characteristics and finding development opportunities. To begin, undertake a self-evaluation or get feedback from others. Self-evaluation might include thinking about your current attitudes and behaviors, motivations, and values and comparing them to what you would like them to be. To get a more detailed overview of your strengths and limitations, seek feedback from others such as friends, family, colleagues, or a mentor. You can find opportunities for growth after you have a thorough awareness of your personality features.

This can include recognizing qualities that you want to improve or habits that you want to change. For example, you might wish to concentrate on becoming more confident, empathetic, or efficient at stress management. Similarly, if you want to improve your communication skills, you may try to actively listen to others for the majority of the conversation and try to actively participate in conversations with others. Set clear, achievable development goals once you've identified areas for improvement. Make certain that your objectives are practical and reachable, and that you have a clear plan in place to achieve them. This can include a timetable for when you want to achieve your goals as well as specific steps you will take to get there.

———

**Do:** It is an obvious thing for us, that we think a lot to undertake many tasks but in reality, we fail to bring the plan into action. This step involves putting your plan into action and changing your habit. Once you start working on the plan, it helps you develop your personality. You can engage in self-improvement activities such as taking training, attending sessions, reading books, or practicing new habits based on your goals. For example, if you are willing to improve your confidence, you may start with a public speaking class, participate in group activities, or engage in regular discussions. Similarly, if you wish to develop your empathy, look for opportunities to volunteer, practice active listening, or participate in empathy training activities.

It is critical to remember that personality development is an ongoing process that requires time and effort to provide long-term benefits. Be persistent and patient in your efforts to create your personality, and keep in mind that improvement is sometimes gradual and incremental.

---

**Check:** The third step is to check your progress toward your objectives as well as the impact of your activities on your overall personality. Many times we underestimate the step of checking and just maintain to continue doing a particular task. Skipping this step of checking your status, makes it difficult for you to know your current state of progress. It involves monitoring the success of your strategy and deciding whether you are making progress toward your objectives or not. In order to measure your development, you can reflect on your thought process, accept the feedback positively from others, and measure the statistics involved. You can try writing a diary in order to track your growth in your desired areas like time management, communication skills, stress management, and empathy. To gain a wide and complete view of how your personality is growing, you can also seek input from others, such as friends, family, or a mentor.It's important to look at both performance and improvements and evaluate them honestly and objectively. This will help you identify what is working well, what needs to be changed, and what new goals need to be set.

---

**Act:** In the step to check, you may come across many things which are needed to be modified to eliminate. In this step, we modify the plan based on progress assessments. Once you're on track, you can continue planning and set new, more challenging goals. If progress is less than expected, you can revise your plan, set new more achievable goals, and devise new strategies to reach those goals.

In this step, you take action to continue the improvement cycle, using what you learned from the previous steps to make adjustments as needed. It is also about being flexible, open to new ideas, and recognizing that there is always room for growth and improvement. The "act" step is about putting into practice the lessons you learned from the previous step and continuously improving your character. to evaluate and modify plans if necessary.

Continuing with the similar example of you being more confident and you have made progress in that area, you can set new, more challenging goals to boost your confidence even more. If so, you may need to revise your plan and set new, more achievable goals. It's important to be adaptable and flexible in your approach and embrace the idea that personal development is an ongoing journey. By repeating the PDCA cycle, you can develop your individuality and continue to grow into your best self.

By following the PDCA framework, you can continuously improve your personality, develop new skills and habits, and achieve your development goals over time.

# PLAN-DO-CHECK-ACT

## Plan

Problem in detail and establish objectives.

Details of the problem and its relevance.

Cause of the problem and points of improvement.

Define the action Plan,

## Do

Execute the steps defined in the action plan.

## Check

Check your status and evaluate results

## Act

Modify the plan based on progress assessments and repeat the cycle

**Notes:**_______________________________________________

Template to practice PDCA

# Building a Better You through Virtues

Building a Better You Through Virtues relates to the view that accepting and implementing certain ethical values and principles might result in personal growth and development. An individual may become a better version of themselves and have a successful life by adopting virtues such as honesty, empathy, confidence, flexibility, trust, forgiveness, kindness, patience, self-discipline, compassion, justice, responsibility, determination, and many more. You can focus on virtues by writing virtues on your calendar randomly on random dates and doing it on a daily basis is an excellent method to develop and strengthen that virtue in your life. Setting aside time each day to focus on a particular virtue can help you develop the habit and apply it into your everyday activities and interactions with others. As you work to live up to your own standards and ideas, this can help you lead a more full and meaningful life. Practicing virtues can also enhance your connections with others and produce inner happiness and satisfaction.

### Honesty

It is the quality of being truthful and plain in one's behavior, speech, and thoughts. It is seen as a necessary virtue in personal and professional interactions because it promotes trust and integrity. Being honest not only helps to develop a good reputation but also allows a person to live with a clean conscience. It promotes open communication since individuals are more willing to express their views and feelings with someone they believe is telling the truth.

Practicing Honesty: I was quite wondering to write an activity to practice honesty because honesty is not the thing you need to read or learn, it should in your nerves. If you are honest then you are honest, and no other side of the coin. It reflects your personality. You can simply engage in regular, open, and honest communication with others. This can involve sharing your thoughts and feelings, asking for feedback, and engaging in active listening and empathy when interacting with others. Additionally, making a conscious effort to avoid dishonesty and to act with integrity in all aspects of life, such as in personal relationships, at work, and in decision-making, can also help to build a culture of honesty and promote greater accountability and transparency in your life.

### Empathy

It is the ability to understand and share the emotions of others. We can understand it by placing ourselves in the shoes of another person. Doing this helps in feeling care and concern for their well-being. I feel it is an important part of emotional intelligence and is essential in developing good feelings connected to others. People who can empathize with one another can resolve issues peacefully and create mutual respect. It also helps for offering assistance to people in need, as well as promote a more caring and understanding community.

Practicing Empathy: Active listening is one practical exercise for incorporating empathy into daily life. This is focusing complete attention to someone when they are speaking, avoiding distractions, and making an attempt to understand their point of view, emotions, and feelings. When practicing in active listening, avoid the tendency to interrupt or ignore the person's opinions and instead try to see their point of view. This can help the growth of empathy by building a better understanding of people and their lives. Doing for community service or doing acts of kindness can also help develop empathy by exposing people to other viewpoints and needs and encouraging them to consider the experiences of others.

One tale I heard in school always comes to me whether I read, write, or exercise empathy. I was motivated to write it and could not stop. A true story of empathy.

One day, a saint went to a river to bath. As he was taking bath, he noticed a scorpion struggling in the water, unable to swim. Being a compassionate and empathetic individual, the saint realized that the scorpion was in danger of drowning and decided to rescue it.

The saint approached the scorpion cautiously, knowing that scorpions have a tendency to attack when they feel threatened. He picked up the scorpion, trying to keep it away from his body, but as soon as he was about to place it on the riverbank, the scorpion stung him on the finger. The sharp pain caused the saint to fling his hand, and the scorpion was thrown back into the water.

Despite the pain, the saint was determined to save the scorpion and tried again. But, each time he tried to rescue the creature, it would sting him, causing him to instinctively fling his hand, and the scorpion would once again be thrown back into the water. This repeated several times until the saint finally managed to save the scorpion.

The saint's disciples were worried for him, watching him struggle and sway from the pain of the multiple stings. They requested the saint to leave the vicious creature and let it fend for itself, but he ignored their pleas and continued his rescue efforts. Eventually, the saint succeeded in saving the scorpion, and the disciples carried him to his hut to tend to his wounds.

Once the saint had regained consciousness, one of his disciples asked him why he let the scorpion attack him multiple times and why he continued to help it. The saint replied, "Tthe scorpion did not sting me out of hatred or bad intentions. It is in the nature of a scorpion to sting. It was not aware of my intentions to help it and kept stinging me because of its limited understanding. But, just as the scorpion could not leave its nature, I could not leave mine, which is to practice empathy and help anyone in need. I should not let the stings from a scorpion prevent me from performing my duty as a savior."

The saint's words serve as a reminder to all of us that we should never let negativity from others affect our actions, thoughts, and words. Instead, we should continue to perform our duties with love and practice empathy in all that we do.

———

### Forgiveness

It is the act of letting go of negative sentiments toward someone who has hurt or mistreated you in some way. It is an important component of human development and well-being since keeping grudges and resentment can lead to bad emotions, stress, and physical health issues. Individuals may break free from the past and move forward in a constructive path through forgiving others.

Practicing Forgiveness: An effective way to practice forgiveness is to engage in a forgiveness exercise, such as writing a letter to the person they need to forgive its ok if you do not send it. Visualization can also help in practicing forgiveness, where you can imagine releasing the negative feelings towards the person and replacing them with feelings of compassion and understanding. I tried this activity of visualization a few years back in a training program. We were told to imagine the person we feel you are having anger, hatred, or grudges for him. After that, we were told to visualize his five good qualities and the incidences when he had helped me by any means.

Then, by remembering his qualities and his kind acts, I forgive him and clean my heart from anger and hatred about him. It was difficult for me to understand how come such simple activity can change my perspective about any person.

———

## Patience

I feel it is an important but difficult virtue to implement in self-transformation because for practicing and making patience a habit, you need to work on it for a very long. It helps a person to continue in the face of difficulties and disappointments while maintaining a positive and consistent attitude toward their goals. It is easy to grow disappointed and give up on the process of self-improvement if one lacks patience, especially when progress is extremely slow or challenges occur. However, with patience, one may stay focused and inspired while making steady progress toward their goal.

Practicing Patience: The activities require you to concentrate on the current time rather than focus on the past or worry about the future. Meditation, deep breathing exercises, or simply paying attention to your environment can all be used to practice it. This can help you become more aware of your thoughts, feelings, and responses, and teach you how to respond to difficult circumstances with calm and patience. Another successful method is to engage in hobbies that demand patience, such as gardening, reading, or a creative pastime such as sketching or painting.

---

## Self-discipline

Self-discipline is a very essential tool of self-transformation. It might be tough to resist distractions, temptations, and undesirable habits and stay focused on your goals if you lack self-discipline. With self-discipline, you can keep your commitments and make progress toward your aim. It helps in maintaining focus and motivation in the face of difficulties or failures. Also, self-discipline allows you to properly manage your time and energy, allowing them to prioritize the most important tasks and avoid spending time on unnecessary activities.

Practicing Self-discipline: Self-discipline is tough as we have a habit of being disciplined forcefully by a teacher, by the boss, by the rules, and by the laws. But practicing self-discipline is a key component of self-transformation. It can be done by establishing and keeping to a daily routine can assist to improve self-discipline and provide structure and regularity in your life. Also prioritizing work and properly managing your time can assist to enhance self-discipline and prevent spending time on ineffective activities. You can also start by accepting responsibility for your behavior and committing to personal development and self-improvement can assist to build self-discipline and encourage good transformation.

## Confidence

As it influences ideas and behaviors, confidence is an important aspect of human growth. It enables you to believe in yourself, take risks, communicate effectively, develop good connections, and overcome challenges. It also promotes mental health, boosts self-esteem, and increases happiness and resilience. Individuals may achieve their goals, form strong bonds, and live satisfying lives by establishing and maintaining confidence.

Practicing Confidence: You can start working on confidence with a simple and easy practice of regularly repeating positive affirmations to yourself, this can help to build confidence and boost self-esteem. You can go on with talking to yourself by seeing in the mirror and then engaging in public speaking or presentation opportunities. while doing so try to be in the surrounding of positive and supportive people. Take criticism as positive feedback and try to be motivated always.

## Responsibility

To achieve success and pleasure, you must accept responsibility for your own actions, choices, and life situations. When you accept responsibility for your life, you give yourself the ability to make modifications and improvements. It also help in avoiding blaming others for your difficulties and learning from your mistakes. Accepting responsibility for your actions shows a high degree of integrity and maturity, and it may gain the respect and trust of others.

Practicing Responsibility: Work hard to Keep your promises and for being dependable in both personal and professional relationships. Also, witness your actions and acknowledge your mistakes and take ownership of your behavior, rather than blaming others or making excuses. Try to manage your time by Planing your day and prioritizing tasks to ensure you meet deadlines and responsibilities. Being proactive is essential for being responsible. You can do it by anticipating problems and taking action to prevent them, rather than waiting for things to happen to you.

## Trust

We can't picture our lives without trust. We trust a number of individuals in our daily lives, such as a taxi driver who will drop us off securely, physicians, chefs, and so on. It establishes the foundation for positive relationships and a sense of security within oneself. Individuals who trust themselves are more likely to make confident decisions, take calculated risks, and hold themselves accountable for their actions. Trusting others enables meaningful connections, open communication, and the ability to rely on loved ones for help in times of need. Individuals who practise trust can cultivate a more positive outlook, reduce stress and anxiety, and live a more fulfilling life overall.

Practicing Trust: Practicing trust in daily life involves lot many similar things as honesty, responsibility, and empathy. Because by enbibing these qualities one can be trustworthy and also can trust others. It can be done by being honest with oneself and others, keeping promises and commitments, being open and transparent in communication, taking accountability for one's actions, and having confidence in oneself and others. It also involves letting go of control and being vulnerable, accepting and appreciating differences, and forgiving both oneself and others. Building trust takes time and effort, but it is essential for building healthy relationships and achieving personal growth.

When I was going through the lessons of Natural Language Processing, I realise that understanding any concept and training the mind becomes easy through reading and visualizing stories related to that specific concept. Here I could not stop myself from writing inspirational story on Trust. A true story of Trust.

A small girl took out her piggy bank from the closet. She poured all the coins from it onto the floor and counted them carefully. She collects all the coins and takes them to the nearby medical Store. She saw people standing to buy medicines. She waited patiently for the pharmacist to give her some attention but he was too busy at this moment. After waiting for some time she makes a noise from the coins he was carrying in her hands. That makes the pharmacist notice her. The Pharmacist asked her, *"And what do you want?"*, She said without waiting for his question. *"I want to talk to you about my brother, He is very sick, and I want to buy a miracle for him so that he could be well again."* The pharmacist was confused and surprised by her reply. He was wondering how come someone buy a miracle.

The pharmacist asked the girl, *"Can you please tell me what miracle you need and why?"* The girl replied *"My brother has some serious issue inside his head and my Daddy says only a miracle can save him now. So, please tell me how much does a miracle cost?"* *"We don't sell miracles here, little girl. I'm sorry but I can't help you,"* the pharmacist said, softening a little. *"Listen, I have the money to pay for it. If it isn't enough, I will get the rest. Just tell me how much it costs."* The pharmacist's brother heard all these conversations, he stooped down and asked the little girl, *"What kind of a miracle does your brother need?"* *"I don't know,"* she replied. *"I just know he's sick and Mommy says he needs an operation. But my Daddy can't pay for it, so I want to use my money."* *"How much do you have?"* asked that man. The showed the coins in her hand and said, *"And it is all the money I have, but I can get some more if I need to."* *"Well, what a coincidence,"* smiled the man. *"These are the exact price of a miracle for little brothers."*

He took her money in one hand and with the other hand he grasped her mitten and said *"Take me to where you live. I want to see your brother and meet your parents. Let's see if I have the miracle you need."* That well-dressed man was a famous surgeon, specializing in neuro-surgery. The operation was completed free of charge and her brother was home again and doing well. Mom and Dad were happily talking about the chain of events that had led them to this place. That surgery," her Mom whispered. *"was a real miracle. I wonder how much it would have cost?"* the little girl smiled. She knew exactly how much a miracle cost... a few coins from the piggy bank, plus the Trust of a little girl.

# The Transformative Practice of Personal Journaling

Personal journaling can be used in a transformative way. Journaling is nothing but writing a daily diary in a simplified and systematic way for a desirable outcome. It can play an important role in personal development by serving as a tool for reflection and self-awareness. During my Neuro-Linguistic Programming (NLP) certifications, I learned about journaling. When I come to know that keeping a daily diary might help in personal growth, I questioned how keeping a personal journal could transform me. Because I have only ever seen daily diaries in classic Bollywood movies, where they were frequently used to expose the suspense at the conclusion. As a result, it increased my curiosity about this idea and how it may be used for self-transformation. As I continued to study it, I discovered the details that set journaling a little different from everyday diary writing and make it more productive.

Writing in a personal journal allows you to reflect on your past experiences, ideas, thoughts, actions, relations, and emotions to better understand who you are and how your life has grown. Thus, it helps to analyze patterns and identify areas for growth and improvement. It can be a place for defining and tracking individual objectives as well as for keeping notes of achievements and mistakes. Additionally, journaling every day may help in self-discovery and the clarity of your values, attitudes, and priorities. Through journaling, we can express ourselves in ways that verbal communication cannot. We can use our diaries to explore our imaginations and capture our ideas, thoughts, and feelings in tangible form. Additionally, journaling can be a powerful tool for self-care and compassion. By taking time to reflect on our experiences, we can learn to be kind and more understanding of ourselves, and develop a more positive self-image.

To start a personal diary, all you need is a diary and a pen. You can set aside a specific time each day to write, or write whenever you feel inspired. The most important thing is, to be honest, and authentic in your writing. There's no right or wrong way to journal, and it's important to remember that there's no pressure to write perfectly. The purpose of personal journaling is to achieve self-awareness and use that awareness to make positive changes in your life. In summary, personal journaling is a valuable practice that can bring many benefits. Through regular journaling, we can deepen our understanding of ourselves, process our emotions in healthy ways, make positive changes in our lives, and develop self-compassion. Try it and see how it can change your life. By taking time to reflect on the things we are grateful for, we can improve our overall health and lead a more fulfilling life.

An example of how personal journaling can be used transformatively is the practice of gratitude journaling. By regularly writing down what you are grateful for, you can move your focus away from negative thoughts and feelings to a more positive attitude. This can lead to an overall increase in well-being and happiness.

To start a gratitude journal, start by writing at a specific time everyday as per your life schedule, such as in the morning or at night. Take a few minutes during this time to reflect on what you are grateful for. These can range from big things like a good job, any award or recognition, or a healthy family to small things like a beautiful sunset, appreciation by the boss, or good tea that made your day. Write them down in your journal and take the time to really enjoy and appreciate them.

As you keep journaling, you may find that your perspective on life begins to change. Instead of focusing on negative thoughts and feelings, you start seeing the world in a more positive way. You are more likely to notice the good things in your life and appreciate and enjoy them.

Additionally, keeping a gratitude journal might help in reducing stress and anxiety. When we're feeling overburdened, it's simple to bring an end to worrying ideas. We may, however, stop this pattern and concentrate on a more positive state of mind by taking the time to reflect on the things for which we are thankful. Maintaining a gratitude journal helps strengthen our bonds with one another. Being thankful for people around us increases our ability to be kind, forgiving, and understanding. Deeper and more genuine connections with those around us may result from it. In summary, gratitude journaling is an effective method that can be used to focus on a more positive state of mind, reduce stress and anxiety, and improve our relationships. ta. By regularly taking time to reflect on the things we are grateful for, we can improve our overall health and lead a more fulfilling life.

You can use the template given below or even can modify the template as per you.

# Gratitude Journal

Date:__________

**2 PERSONS**
I am thankful today

1.___________________

2.___________________

**2 THINGS**
I am thankful today

1.___________________

2.___________________

**2 Good incidences that happened today**

1._______________________________________________

2._______________________________________________

**2 Qualities of me helped me today**

Qualities

1.___________________

2.___________________

How they helped

1.___________________

2.___________________

NOTES:

Template for Gratitude Journal

There are many types of journaling, each with its own purposes and benefits. Here are some examples:

Gratitude journaling: This type of journaling involves regularly writing down things for which you are grateful. For example, every day you could write in your diary something or someone that you appreciate or something that makes you happy. This type of journaling can help you focus on a more positive mindset.

Reflection journaling: Journaling for reflection is looking back on your past experiences, ideas, and emotions to achieve new understanding. For example, you can consider and write about a specific incident that happened during the day, week, or month in your diary. This can help you in seeing the way of your respond and reaction to each situation.

Goal journaling: This type of journaling involves writing down your short-term and long-term goals and analyzing them to derive ideas for their accomplishment. You can note down the things that go well and takes you nearer to your goal, and also make a regular note of the things which act as an obstacle in the path of fulfillment of your goal. You can analyze these things.

Travel journaling: This type of journal is useful to capture your experiences during your trip, such as different locations you have seen, people you have met there and during the journey, and activities you have done and observed. For example, you may write about the view and good things of a new region, as well as your opinion and feelings about the experience. It allows you to lock the memories, improve your observations, think about your experiences, and absorb the good and positive aspects of diverse cultures and places.

Creativity journaling: This type of journaling is used to express your creativity, through writing, drawing, painting or by any other way. For example, you try to create a personal and artistic representation of your thoughts, your goal, and feelings. Creative journaling can help you tap into your imagination, explore your emotions, and develop your artistic skills.

These are just a few examples of the many different types of journaling available. The key is to find a type of journaling that resonates with you and fits your needs. You can also experiment with different types of journaling to see which one works best for you.

# CHAPTER FIFTEEN

# The 26 Steps of Self Transformation

## Adapt the Adaptability

A crucial component of self-transformation is the practice of adaptability. You need to be willing to change your thoughts and methods to get the results you want, much like a chameleon changes its color to blend in with its environment. By accepting adaptability, you gain a sense of flexibility and openness, allowing for development and progress. Being fearless and self-aware is necessary for this activity because it includes stepping well beyond your comfort zone.

## Be Brave

I feel bravery is not about having no fear, but having victory over it. Being brave means acceptance to change and stretching the limits as wide as you can. It is also about facing your fears of transformation and weaknesses and making them your strengths. By taking charge of your life and molding it as per your desire, you set out on a path of personal development and progress that pushes you to evolve into your finest version.

## Care for others and Care for yourself

You need to maintain a proper balance between caring for others and caring for yourself. This will take you ahead in your journey of self-transformation. Caring for others and giving a helping hand to others helps in building good connections and strengthening relationships. While taking care of yourself, you become more emotionally and mentally strong. By this, you will be able to take hard decisions and face the change. Find the balance between these two, and you'll set the foundation for lasting and fulfilling self-transformation.

## Do with Determination

Self-transformation is driven by determination. It is a strong commitment to work for your goal despite any difficulties or failures that may come your way. With strong willpower, you can get over the difficulties and worries that prevent you from reaching your goals. Even if the road ahead is dark and nothing is visible to you, determination of reaching the goal will propel you to keep moving forward and to channelise your inner strength for use. It is just like moving forward, one step at a time until you get where you desired to be.

## Express Yourself

Expression itself is the language, the language having the potential to establish a connect. It is simply letting your thoughts, feelings, and desires flow freely, without any restrictions. You can discover the real you by expressing yourself. Self-expression is an efficient way of self-transformation because it helps you to find and understand your own self, to take off the masks, and to feel more confident. You may learn to love and accept yourself for who you are, just as you are in the real sense, just by expressing yourself.

## Find Happiness Through Forgiveness

Forgiveness can move you in peace by helping to heal the wounds of the past. Your act of forgiving will help you to let go grudges, which will set you free from the constraints of bitterness. By forgiving you can witness that you have released the sorrow and thus you provide space for your transformation. It will be your brave journey of self-discovery, face your own failures and weaknesses, and show others kindness. You can definitely recover your power, change your lives, and discover a way to inner peace through forgiveness.

## Give with Heart

By the act of giving from the heart, you start your journey of personal transformation. It is a path that results in a strong appreciation of the value of giving and the satisfaction that comes from improving the lives of others. When you give from the heart, you let go of your own ego and adopt an attitude of generosity, knowing that by giving of yourselves and your resources, you spread happiness throughout society. You remove layers of ego with each act of kindness and move closer to a sense of belonging.

## Have a Healthy life

You should be committed to put your health first as you set out on your journey of self-transformation. Go ahead with taking care of yourself by eating healthful meals, working out frequently, and practicing self-care. You can achieve internal harmony while maintaining the delicate balance between your physical, emotional, and mental health. You can better control your future, develop resilience, and increase your happiness by leading a healthy lifestyle.

## Involve Yourself

Involving helps you to know the concept with depth and to extend the perspectives. To truly transform yourself, it is imperative to involve yourself fully in the process. You need to realise that being away from anything will not let you get the essence of it. You need to be fully into it, it will help to activate your senses. You must be practicing involvement, especially when you are trying out new things, this will help you to understand and implement it in a better way. Many times it helps for yourselves to break your comfort, and realise your full potential.

## Just be Joyfull

If you want an everlasting transformation then you should realise that the transformation should be inside-out. By practicing joyfulness you can experience yourself more brightened and more peaccful. You can send away all your tensions and worries by concentrating on joy. Just close your eyes, take a breath, experience the grace with you, remember the fortunes, and you will experience a smile on your face, with a wave of joy inside. It will direct you towards your development and new opportunities, and also will make you enjoy the little things and feel surrounded by good vibes.

## Know your limits

If you wish to extend your limits you must first know your limits. For self-transformation, you must be aware of your weaknesses and limitations. To grow and improve, you must first be aware of where you stand. This practice requires patience and courage to face your limitations. By being aware of your limits, you can avoid disappointment and focus on steady progress toward becoming your best self.

## Live with Logics

Be Logical and reasonable, this will be a crucial form of transformation for you. Instead of taking your decisions and actions on the basis of emotions, use your logical and critical thinking. This will help you in decision-making and avoid confusion. By developing a logical and rational mindset, you will be better prepared to face obstacles with assurance and clarity, creating a route that is sustainable for your own personal development and satisfaction.

## Motivate Yourself

Sometimes motivation from others acts like rainwater, it comes, it strikes, and it flows away. Thus, you can notice that it does not last for a longer time. But self-motivation is a powerful tool of self-transformation. It helps you to use the inner thrust to drive yourself toward your dreams. You will develop a confident and determined attitude by making yourself your biggest supporter and source of motivation. Nothing can prevent you from achieving your goals if self-motivation is your driving force.

## Nurture your skills

Identifying your skills, developing new skills, and nurturing them, will take out a better version of yourself. Do not underestimate the value of developing your talents. Spend some time expanding your knowledge, pushing yourself, and taking development chances. You'll prepare the way for a long-lasting and pleasant transformation if you put effort into yourself and keep developing your skills. Develop your abilities so you may enjoy the benefits in all areas of your life and make the most of your path to transformation.

## Open the door of Opportunity

On your way to transformation, open new doors to opportunities without hesitation. Go against the resistance, accept change, and take chances. You will learn new things, develop in new ways, and achieve new heights if you do this. Never stop aiming for the stars and keep your heart and mind open. This strategy will enable you to get the most out of your path to self-transformation and build a life that is full of limitless opportunities.

## Practice Professionalism

Accept professionalism as a virtue and practice it every day. Develop a professional and committed attitude toward your behavior and communication. Every single step you take towards professionalism—from preparing for success to showcasing good communication skills to your personal development and helps you become the finest form of yourself. Give yourself the knowledge, expertise, and self-assurance you need to achieve your targets and create a lasting impact on the world.

## Question yourself

Dare to question yourself. The doors of your personal development and transformation may be unlocked through the power of introspection. Challenge your principles and beliefs, ask yourself difficult questions, and enjoy the self-discovery process. You may develop a better awareness of who you are and make significant adjustments that will have beneficial for improving yourself.

## Respond instead of Reacting

Make the decision to respond with intention and kindness when faced with challenges in life. A downward loop and personal progress can be separated by the gap between reacting and responding. Breathe deeply, collect your thoughts, and face every circumstance with a cool and calm head. Therefore, respond rather than react, and see how you change into a more composed and confident person.

## Simplify your lifestyle

The height of luxury is simplicity. Simplify your priorities and simplify your life. Simplifying your lifestyle will help you live a stress-free life. Just organize your responsibilities, manage your physical and mental space, and get away from distractions. You make room for development and introspection by simplifying your way of living. Accept the calm and clarity that come with living a simpler life, and see how this will make you more conscious, content, and deliberate.

## Think twice, then act once

It is rightly said, "Think twice, then act once." Take some time and think about your action and its impact on you. Thinking more broadly can serve as the platform for bringing on the change you want to see in yourself. By practicing it, you will never regret your actions as you will already consider your choices carefully and the impact they will have on your development before taking any action. Follow your instincts, but also believe in the value. Believe that every action is important and watch it closely and accept the feedback.

## Understand the Unconcious mind

Do not undervalue the unconscious mind's power as you begin your journey of self-transformation. It unlocks a lot of our most basic wants, worries, and emotions. Take the time to explore the depths of your unconscious mind in order to genuinely know yourself and promote progress. Allow your inner feelings and thoughts to arise by studying them. Then and only then will you be able to see clearly and take charge of any unconscious practices that could be preventing your transformation.

## Versatility should be your signature style

Allow versatility to be your guiding principle on the path to self-transformation. You should work on developing a wide range of skills and viewpoints and always continue the learning approach. You need to play various roles in your life, and for this, you should view problems from many perspectives and come up with original solutions. Your versatility will grow in value as you develop, and helps you to successfully deal with life's ups and downs.

## Write your own destiny

Remember that you have the power to write your own destiny. The future is in your hands, and you have the pen. Dream big, make plans, and don't be afraid to lead your own way. Take steps to make your dreams a reality by believing in your own capacity and your own skill. And as you keep developing and growing, you'll discover that the future you once imagined for yourself actually comes true. So take control of the tale, my friend, and write it with passion, purpose, and perseverance.

## X-factor

Identify and develop your own X-factor. It is necessary for self-transformation. You stand out from the crowd because of this unique feature of yours, which you may utilise for your advantage, for realising your potential, and for reaching your goals. It might be a skill, ability, or personality characteristic that you've always had or that you've acquired through time. It can be your sense of humour, your communication skills, or your determination and ambition. Accept it and make the best of it.

## Yes, you can!

Have faith in your skills and know that "Yes, you can!", you can go through any difficulty and overcome any obstacle. Have confidence in yourself and never forget that you have the ability to change and mould yourself into the person you wish. Although the route may be challenging, the end result is worthwhile. You possess the fortitude, tenacity, and resilience needed to bring about change.

## Zero tolerance for excuses

Zero tolerance for excuses should be your thumb rule of living life. Let go of the excuses you give yourself for not being able to or not wishing to execute anything. Rather, concentrate on figuring out how to make it happen. Excuses are only obstacles in the way of achievement and prevent you from realising your full potential. So overcome them and recognise the strength of willpower and initiative and hold yourself accountable and reject excuses.

# ACT NOW, *Transform* FOREVER